A True Survival Guide for Small Businesses

A True Survival Guide for Small Businesses

◆

A no-nonsense approach to successful retailing

Michael Ruffino

iUniverse, Inc.
New York Bloomington Shanghai

A True Survival Guide for Small Businesses
A no-nonsense approach to successful retailing

iUniverse books may be ordered through booksellers or by contacting:

iUniverse
1663 Liberty Drive
Bloomington, IN 47403
www.iuniverse.com
1-800-Authors (1-800-288-4677)

Because of the dynamic nature of the Internet, any Web addresses or links contained in this book may have changed since publication and may no longer be valid.

The views expressed in this work are solely those of the author and do not necessarily reflect the views of Wild Bird Centers of America, the publisher, and the publisher hereby disclaims any responsibility for them.

ISBN: 978-0-595-47241-3 (pbk)
ISBN: 978-0-595-91523-1 (ebk)

Printed in the United States of America

Dedicated to the memory of my mother,
Phyllis Ruffino,
1929–2001
and
to my in-laws,
Bob and Bev Charlton.
Thank you for all your support and for letting me marry your incredible
daughter.

Contents

Preface

This book will equip you with the necessary tools for marketing, selling, and managing your own store. You will learn from others and take advantage of decades of experience in retail operations to aid you in creating a profitable bottom line sooner.

The pressures and the stress that you will undergo can, at times, be avoided. I have read many self-help books, ranging in type from motivational to economic. But, to tell you the truth, even when I picked up a morsel or two from them, they really didn't help me come up with practical solutions for surviving the early years of retail store ownership.

Who wants to read three hundred pages about finance when the topic can be covered in just a few? I recently read a book that had some salient points about marketing, but it was such a bore! This author spent 80 percent of his time trying to convince me that he was smart and knew more pithy sayings than I did before he got to the really meaty portion of the information. This book is short and to the point. I can't stand it when people talk in circles; it makes me dizzy.

In the first two years of a new business, there are marketing and budgetary challenges that one does not expect; thus, help is needed. The average new store owner fails to make the best choices in marketing, salesmanship, and budgeting. We all have made mistakes, and if you can afford to weather through these errors, then you will be the wiser about avoiding them next time. This book will take you on a journey of successes and failures that you will learn from, and you will find out that it is easier to learn from others' mistakes rather than your own. The solutions found here will create a more successful business with a greater return on your investment.

The illusion that you can open the doors to a new business and instantly make money is quickly broken by the harsh reality that hard work, practical tools, and determination are needed.

Your "mental toughness" will be tested to its limit.

My goal is to give you the lessons I and others learned and to provide solutions that have proved effective. You will come away with a better strategy for success.

Introduction

This book will help new business owners not only beat the odds but also enjoy the process of owning their own business. It is said that 90 percent of new businesses fail in the first two years. That statistic is entirely wrong! According to the latest Small Business Administration survey, only 44 percent of small businesses fail in the first two years. This same survey indicates that once a business has made it five years, it's pretty much in the clear; there is a failure rate of only 2–3 percent after this time.

My wife, Kathy, and I own a small business in Fresno, California, and have recently won a national award for public relations and marketing. Our store trend shows dramatic increases both in profitability and market share. You will find, as we have, that simple plans bring greater performance.

I was promoted to my first management position, at a locally owned video retail store in Modesto, California, at the age of twenty. At twenty-three, I was a manager of three locally owned camera specialty stores in the same town. These stores catered more to the professional than the consumer, but it was here that I began to get the feel for running a small business. After three years there, I was recruited by a "big box" (A large multimillion-dollar departmentalized store) company specializing in the retailing of middle- to high-end electronics.

I eventually worked my way up through every department and position, including a spot in operations, where I learned a lot about a business's P&L (Profit and Loss). This store did about $12 million annually when I took over the reigns as general manager. I spent sixteen years of my life with this company, mostly in Fresno, California.

So what happened? A larger company bought ours for the real estate. When seventeen of our top-producing stores were converted to the new company, thus becoming a whole new store using a different name, I knew the future. We as a company of eighty stores could not maintain a profitable P&L with losing seventeen prime locations.

It was then that I began looking for a different future. Yes, competitors offered me positions that paid well into the six figures. I obviously considered these seriously, but I wanted more for my family than an uncertain corporate future.

My in-laws used to live in Sacramento, California, where they shopped at a local nature store, the Wild Bird Center. At first they suggested buying the store themselves and, since they were close to retiring, having me manage it. I informed them of some very sobering truths about running a business, the initial financial losses, the time and resources needed to keep the business running, and then the wage I needed to support my family. Well, that nixed that idea for them. Then they looked at me and said, "How about you opening the store?" *Hmmm!* I thought about it and discussed it with Kathy. She and my in-laws seemed to think I was capable and that it would be a natural next step in my career. I agreed.

At first, I did not think a bird-watching store was a good idea. What of the market? Was it sufficient to support the business? What about Fresno? What about California? How much money would it cost? A lot of questions had to be answered before I could enter this venture.

The Internet is an amazing thing. As you will agree, the information you need is there, if only you have the patience to find it. A good example: I discovered Department of Agriculture statistics about this hobby on their Web site. The figures floored me, to say the least. In California alone, nearly $2 billion is spent annually on backyard bird-feeding. Evidently, Californians spend more on this hobby than do people in any other state in the union. This fact alone swayed me.

I then contacted both organizations that focus on this hobby, and only one impressed me—the Wild Bird Centers of America (WBCA). Why? One, they responded to my inquiry the next day, whereas the other organization took a week. Two, they wanted to know about me, not my financials. Next, they sent me a franchise pack immediately; I never got one from the other company. WBCA had an inventory control system in place through their computerized point-of-sale (POS) system, while the other franchise still worked on cash registers. In addition, WBCA was introducing the second generation of their POS. A POS system is huge in running a business; the time you save by managing inventory electronically is immeasurable. And, finally, I liked the people I spoke with. George Petrides, Sr., the founder of the franchise, sent me an autographed copy of the *Petersons Field Guide to Trees*, for which his father wrote. That was the seal on the deal.

We visited WBCA in Glen Echo, Maryland, and both parties were impressed with each other and pursued the relationship.

Where do you put a store? "Location, location, location!" is the mantra of the commercial world. I knew Fresno very well and had conducted business here for sixteen years, so I already had a spot in mind. George Petrides Jr. flew out to help me pick a location.

All shopping centers have packets they give to prospective tenants with statistics on traffic counts and the businesses already in place. I wanted an affordable storefront facing a busy street, on the going-home side (the side of the street used mostly for commuters going home), with a strong anchor that had a demographic similar to our store. The franchise worked a miracle in negotiating a contract that gave us one of the lowest rents in the shopping center, for which I am indebted to them.

I wanted to open the store the day after Thanksgiving, the busiest shopping day of the year, but, alas, the tenant in my spot did not vacate in time. I finally got the keys on December 12, 2005, and the very next day we started the needed renovations.

We must have set some sort of record for taking an office spot, tearing down a wall, and creating a backyard nature store in just twelve days. Yes, you heard me right: twelve days! The pebble path, murals, fixtures, paint, and inventory all in twelve days. We were tired and excited.

We opened on December 26, 2005, with what we call a "soft" opening. Besides the banner out front and balloons, there was no other announcement that we were opening on this date. Why? Well, to give us time to get our bugs out. At the time, I knew *nothing* about bird-watching or the difference between a sparrow and a starling. We also needed to learn the POS system before our scheduled grand opening two weeks later.

We took in a total of six hundred dollars that year—over a whole five days!

This book will show you successful formats for marketing; take note of these and translate these ideas into practical goals for your business. Take heed of the failures and the reasons they did not work. Avoid falling into the trap of a skillful sales pitch from the advertiser. Understand that a comfortable amount of working capital can quickly disappear with poor decision-making and poor planning.

The principles outlined in the coming chapters will help you develop your own unique footprint and to create a culture within your four walls that best reflects you.

After all is said and done, you will learn that with shared wisdom comes great peace and fortune.

1

The Basics

After running a retail store for over twenty years, I thought I knew exactly what to expect. I was wrong!

I have grown to deeply respect the small business owner. The fortitude of these individuals is second to none. The bravery to risk it all is admirable. The ability to adapt is commendable. Yes, the small business owner is a rare breed.

UNDERSTAND THE CHALLENGES AHEAD

When you lay the groundwork for opening your own store, ideally you set enough money aside to support the initial growth period. The leading cause of new business failures is this: not enough capital to sustain the early years, the first three years of your business. You must assume you will earn nothing during this time and even lose money initially. However, in the first three years you will experience growth in a way you will perhaps never experience again.

Your first year is relatively poor in gross revenue. It is in the first year that most businesses fail because of unrealistic expectations and poor planning. You see, we expect that our store is such a great idea that *everybody* will buy from it, that success will be speedy and certain. This is a viewpoint destined for failure. In most small businesses, the first year is wrought with stress and financial hardships.

Being prepared for a tough initial road is realistic and a sign of smart planning. If you break even in your second year, you did better than most new businesses. You can see that an owner's dream can quickly crash into a nightmare if somebody doesn't sober him up about the reality of the first years. Having a padded bank account is essential to survival, as are a strict budget, a marketing plan, and the skills to succeed in your new venture.

Your second and third years are so much better. You should expect 25–45 percent growth in these years. Woo hoo! Yep, you're riding high in these years—or are you? Still, most businesses fail because of false expectations and poor planning. Running a business requires serious work and effort. Now, mind you, this can easily be coupled with enthusiastic passion and fun. I don't want to make it sound horribly hard. In fact, if it's done right, it is relatively easy.

Most of my stress as a new business owner came from not knowing what to do or what was coming next. This guide is designed to lower your stress and give you the joy you were looking for when you opened your new business.

You will draw customers mostly from a ten-mile radius of your store.

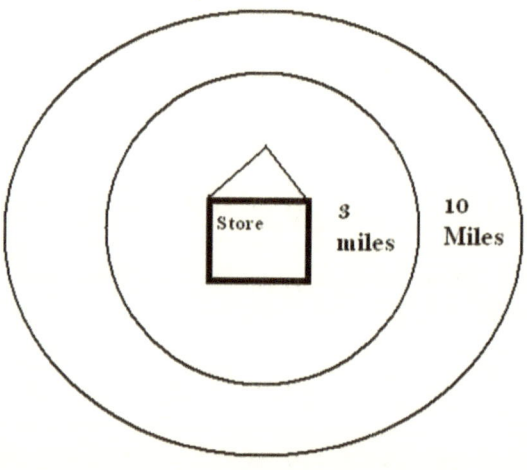

Think about this for a minute: where do you personally shop? Typically, it is somewhere close to where *you* live. It's true that the farther *you* are away from a location, the less effective the draw is. Within a three-mile radius, you will get a much better return from these consumers. Any farther than ten miles, and you will get a much lower return on your investment.

Focus within this three-mile radius initially and you are more likely to get off to a quick start. Then, as traffic builds, you can increase your area of focus to the ten-mile ring. Don't be suckered into the mass media. All mass media advertisers promise the world, yet few can deliver.

These early years are for establishing and growing your business. Marketing during this time is more intense because you are new and trying to create an inroad to your demographic.

WHAT IS A DEMOGRAPHIC?

This is important. You need to understand who your primary customers will be. Male or female? What age group? Blue collar, white collar, or retired? Home owners? Families with children or not? And so on.

The nice thing about being part of a franchise or at least contacting a franchise is that they have all this information. You also could search on the Internet for demographics about the business you are in or are about to open. I found a Department of Agriculture report that detailed all I needed to start with. I then surveyed my customers through e-mail eighteen months after opening to fine-tune my demographic information. I used *Constant Contact* (www. constantcontact.com) to facilitate the survey. This was free to use and allowed me to fine-tune our target demographic. This is crucial in laying the groundwork both for building out and marketing your store.

For instance, our demographic is primarily forty-to-sixty-five-year-old women in a professional occupation or retired. They are homeowners, and many have grandchildren or are raising a family. Now, what can you do with this information? A lot!

The diversity of the product mix needs to cater to these women, and the store's environment needs to be attractive to them, with soft colors, pleasant sounds, and a sitting area. We have a dedicated room for children that we call our "Kid's Corner," where children can play in an area that has product just for them. In that room we conduct events like puppet shows and crafts.

What about advertising? You wouldn't advertise on a hard rock or R&B radio station to capture the attention of this demographic. No, you would choose a soft rock or easy listening station, maybe even an old-time rock and roll station. If you choose to run an ad in your local paper, the garden section would be the wise choice for this group of customers.

The verbiage in your ad needs to take into consideration your target audience. Talk *to* them, not *at* them, and never *down* to them. Make sure your offer is attractive to them. Later, when we discuss advertising, you will see how this can be done.

Knowing your demographic is crucial to success!

These first years for your store are quite a ride, to say the least. The growth is incredible, the stress is intense, and the learning curve is pronounced. But you *can* succeed.

At all times, you need to grow your client base while coming up with new and innovative ways to do so. You need to keep a written record of all of your ad campaigns—which ones succeeded and which ones didn't—so you don't make the same mistake twice.

Although this road is challenging, it is not impossible to navigate. Yes, you need to have enough money (capital) to survive the early years. You also can see that knowing who your customers will be can greatly help you intelligently market yourself and your business.

The next chapter will prove vital to everyone who wants to succeed in any avenue in life, especially in retail and business ownership.

2

Goal-Setting

Goals create focus and purpose. Understanding how to set meaningful goals will allow you to move forward toward your purpose, a self-sustaining business venture.

Now, in order to do this effectively, you must first think about the end result you want—for instance, raising the average invoice a set dollar amount.

The next part of planning is the fun part: brainstorm on the many ways you can do this, through merchandising, training, advertising, up-selling (stepping a customer to a more expensive item), and so on. After coming up with one or two ideas, now you can create a plan to initiate these in a timeline. For instance, if additional training is your goal, when and how will you accomplish it? If your focus is merchandising, what will be the "what, where, and when" of your plan?

You probably already know this acronym, but creating a "SMART" goal is wise.

- **S**pecific—Have details you can accomplish and measure.

- **M**easurable—Don't make a goal like "I want to be the best so-and-so." How can you measure that?

- **A**ttainable—Make the goal reasonable; don't create a goal of increasing business 200 percent.

- **R**ealistic—Create a sales goal that is reasonable. A good example of this would be increasing gross sales 15 percent or increasing the volume of a category proportionately.

- **T**ime measurable—Create a timetable for achieving your goal.

Creating a SMART goal really isn't too difficult. It's just linear thinking, going from point B to point A. You need to break down what seems to be a complex beast to its simplest components and then create processes to accomplish these simpler secondary goals.

Steps in creating a SMART goal:

- First, come up with an ultimate goal.

- Then, think about what needs to happen before that goal becomes a reality. There may be several things that have to fall in place; list these. These are now your secondary goals.

- You then have to look at each of these secondary goals and break them down, reducing them to their simplest components.

- Now, you create a step-by-step process for accomplishing each component.

- Create a timeline for each of these processes; the secondary goals will fall into place as these are accomplished.

- Do not forget to have checkpoints so you can gauge progress and adjust any plan to new circumstances. Creating a flexible plan will reduce many frustrations.

- As each of the secondary goals is accomplished, your ultimate goal will be realized. See Appendix A.

Now you will have to give yourself a reasonable amount of time to secure the desired outcome, with regular check-ins so you can tweak the plan if need be.

Here's a good example of this process. Say I want to increase my average transaction from forty to forty-five dollars by the end of June, and right now it's early April. I will accomplish this with better attachment selling.

Attachment selling is something all of us are familiar with, especially at our local drive-through. The kid on the speaker inevitably asks, "Would you like fries with that?" or "Would you like to super-size your order?" It is simply the suggestion of an appropriate accessory to accompany your order. Attachment selling is done through daily workshops with staff and better merchandising—in other words, displaying an appropriate accessory next to each primary purchase. A good example of this in retail stores is placing cables, batteries, and remotes next to electronic devices, or, in my own case, placing seed next to feeders.

To accomplish our goal, we will do follow-ups every other Thursday until June 30. The plan is:

- **S**pecific ($5 increase per ticket on average);

- Measurable (assuming you have a point-of-sale [POS] system that can give you the information you need);

- Attainable (seems to be with the strategy of attachment selling);

- Realistic (incorporating training and better merchandising); and

- Measured in Time (June 30, with every-other-Thursday follow-up).

Now, an example of poor goal-setting is: "I want to create more profit by working harder." This goal has no clear path, with no road map to a specific goal.

In order for you to understand the principle of a measurable road map to a goal, I have included a simple exercise in Appendix B. This appendix will help you recognize what is a SMART goal and what is not.

Every step you take on your course should follow this pattern. In fact, my plan is nothing new; just about every organization teaches this method of setting goals. I did not invent this, I just borrowed it, and I use it so much that it has come to feel natural to me.

VISIBLY DISPLAY YOUR CURRENT SMART GOALS

Back in 1989, when my previous company recruited me, they trained my colleagues and me in goal-setting. They made each of us write out a SMART goal and then display it prominently where we could see it every day. Some made personal goals and put them on the refrigerator or bathroom mirror; some made business goals and displayed them on their desk or lockers at work. Regardless, we all saw our goals every day and were reminded of them, which helped us stay focused. This may seem silly, but it works; try it.

Next, create a file in your file cabinet with the track record of each of your SMART goals. A personal organizer is a necessity. It can be in the form of a Palm Pilot if you're into technology, or, if you're not, a simple pocket calendar will do. A desk calendar is also helpful; every time you sit at your desk, you are reminded of tasks and goals. You will have so much on your plate that it's easy to forget to do something, like pay bills or give a seminar. Believe me, investing in a personal organizer is a must for reducing stress.

By creating specific, measurable, attainable, realistic, and time-managed goals, we can better see our progress and understand how to attain our desired end result: success.

3

Launching the Business

Now, mind you, I came from a "big box" store with annual sales of $12 million, so spending money on advertising was something with which I was intimately familiar. It was especially fun because it was the corporation's money I was spending.

My lessons on local marketing really started with the "big box" company I worked for. With eighty locations, they had gross revenue of $800 million annually. In their profitable days, they advertised a lot on television. As a company, they attributed too much of their success to that medium.

Early on, the company was customer-centric. The customer came first in the company's early years; if the customer was unhappy, that was unacceptable. They used the famous Nordstrom model as their own. This model is a fairly simple one but is evidently difficult for most companies to grasp—"The customer comes first, no matter what." In this model, not only are the customers right all the time, but they are pampered and assisted in a reverential manner. This really was the reason for my previous company's success early on.

BECOMING A PART OF THE COMMUNITY

The company I worked for started in San Francisco and thus had a lot of ties to the community there. That company preached sincere care for its employees' families and for those in the community. This feeling of community is what generates sales and loyalty. This feeling needs to be marketed above all else. Doing so will set you apart from everyone else, especially your biggest competitor. A good example of this was in 1989 when the Bay-area earthquake hit; the company sprang into action, distributing needed supplies, radios, flashlights, and more to the victims, all for free.

As time rolled by, our company grew from twenty stores when I was hired to eighty stores before they were bought out. During this time, the company lost focus on the community and started focusing on the bottom line. They went from being customer-centric to operating with a bottom-line mentality. This error is repeated over and over again in businesses as they grow larger. The monetary prosperity they obtain blinds them to what gave them their success—the customer.

The store I worked at here in Fresno benefited from a genius of a marketer, Rich Kelly. Rich remembered that community involvement makes a good business great. He and I agreed wholeheartedly on this. I being Yoda's apprentice, the master taught me how to use public icons to our advantage. By attaching ourselves to our demographic's respected organizations, we in turn received respect. By contributing to meaningful causes within the neighborhood, we gained a loyalty exceeding any of our competitions. Rich loved marketing. He is a baby kisser and a WOO-er (Winning Others Over) of people. Watching him work his magic for the store was great.

HOW TO BECOME PART OF THE COMMUNITY

- When picking a group or organization to affiliate with, choose one that is of interest to your demographic.

- Contact local clubs like the Kiwanis, Elks Lodge, American Legion, etc.

- Join the Chamber of Commerce and become active in it, not a passive member.

- Contribute to nonprofit groups like the zoo, industry-specific clubs (in our case, the Audubon Society and the like), or outreach programs for the handicapped or indigent.

- Work with animal shelters and like groups that have strong emotional ties.

- Participate with Girl and Boy Scouts and other youth organizations.

- Work with local sport teams, college or professional.

- Contribute to your unified school system and your city's Parks and Recreation Department.

You must adopt this principle of community in order to market in the most effective way possible.

When you start your business, you need to attach yourself to other local organizations that are respected in the community.

Why? They have an established membership list and carry a measure of respect in the public eye. Attaching yourself to them instantly transfers that respect to you and your store. This is called networking, a term that has a multitude of facets.

I wanted the grand opening of our Wild Bird Center store to be sensational! I contacted local groups, the Fresno Audubon Society, the Riverparkway Trust (a local reclamation-of-habitat group), and the Chaffee Zoo. They all agreed to attend our opening. This was crucial for the success of the next step: press releases.

I sent out press releases to all the media organizations: TV stations, newspapers large and small, radio stations, and private organizations, all through the Internet. This was easy, since they all had Web sites with a link for press releases.

Here is what we released:

For Immediate Press Release

Contact: Michael and Katherine Ruffino
Owners
Wild Bird Center
1075 E. Bullard

Fresno CA, 93710
559-432-WILD

New Wild Bird Center Lands in Fresno
Local Organizations Migrate to Their Grand Opening

(Date—Fresno, CA)—Valley birders have a new place to migrate for all their wild birding supplies. Local residents Michael and Kathy Ruffino have recently opened Wild Bird Center, a wild bird supply store, in Fresno. The grand opening reflects the growing trend of bird-watching in the valley. During the grand opening from January 6th to 8th, attendees will include the River Parkway and the Audubon Society, with guests and presenters from the Chaffee Zoo.

According to the U.S. Fish and Wildlife Service, nearly 26 million Californians fed, photographed, and observed wildlife in 2001. And they didn't necessarily travel to do it. Nearly 3.8 million Californians have bought food to feed birds and other wild animals around their home.

Michael Ruffino, co-owner with his wife Kathy, says regarding this trend, "Birding is one of the fastest-growing outdoor activities in America. We are fortunate to have many beautiful birds here in Fresno, and our goal is to help our neighbors attract and enjoy them."

Area bird-watchers can spot quality birding and outdoor living products in the store. The Wild Bird Center holds an exclusive line of MoBi (short for More Birds) mesh feeders, specially formulated birdseed blends, and a beautiful collection of birding ensembles. For those wanting a more decorative approach, the Ruffinos offer outdoor fountains and garden art. Nature enthusiasts can receive help choosing a binocular and even find creative gift ideas, such as garden accessories, CD's, stationery, nature books, decorative novelty items, and even environmentally conscious, organic coffees and tea.

"Our Wild Bird Center products are top performers in scientific tests," notes Kathy. "We combine our high-end product line with a solid knowledge in birding. Bird-feeding recommendations are based on documented research describing what, where, and how birds like to eat. And customers can pick up our free bimonthly newsletter, Wild Bird News. This great resource offers feeding tips, bird-friendly landscaping ideas, regional bird news, and new products."

For both novices and aficionados, the Ruffinos will sponsor store events such as bird walks, workshops, and educational programs. This Wild Bird Center is a much-needed resource for an area that has starved for such a commodity. Since it's the only store of its kind in the central valley, no wonder everyone is flocking to the Wild Bird Center.

PRESS RELEASE FORMAT

- Contact information goes on the top left.

- Write a direct and interesting title.

- The first paragraph should include a brief overview of the event.

- Include a couple of paragraphs detailing the event in brief. Give readers a reason to contact you by piquing their interest.

- The concluding paragraph should be a summation of the event and an invitation for people to contact you for more details.

You can see why this press release got the media's attention. Having other locally respected groups come to our grand opening created an immediate respect for our little store. The newspaper did a full spread on our store; the local NBC affiliate did five live spots during the entire week, with teasers about our store's grand opening; and the opening events were included on newspaper and online community calendars.

Wow! Imagine having to pay for all of that. It was like tripling my advertising budget—and I got it all for *free*!

YOUR SUPPLIERS WILL HELP YOU!

I would also recommend firmly asking all of your vendors (suppliers) for a free giveaway item to be sent with your opening orders. Vendors will be happy to accommodate this request. You can generate excitement by having hourly giveaways in your store. Make a big deal about it when pulling the raffle ticket, and make an announcement five to ten minutes prior to every drawing. People will stay—and the longer they stay, the more likely they are to buy something.

So that took care of the free stuff. Since free publicity can be a crapshoot, I had to spend money to assure myself of success. You need to keep track of the coupons you distribute in your ad campaign in a way that gives you information to help you make smart marketing decisions in the future.

CREATING AN ATTRACTIVE CAMPAIGN

- Your ads should be in full color.

- Coupons should be specific, with easy-to-understand wording.

- The offer should be attractive. A giveaway is best; we will discuss this in more detail in chapter 7.

- Most offers should be time bound as a rule—have an expiration date. If you choose to break this rule as I do for many of my campaigns, make sure that incentives are scheduled, like events, giveaways, programs, and the like for the consumer to visit within a timely manner. These events will cause most to redeem your coupons on your schedule.

- The disclaimers could be as simple as: "Cannot be combined with any other offers" and "See store for details."

- Coupon postcards should be oversized. This makes them stand out in the mail.

- Use each customer's name in the address. A list of names and addresses can be purchased from another company, which we will discuss a little later under the subheading *Creating a Direct Mail Campaign.*

I strongly recommend using a sophisticated Point of Sale (POS) system. A computerized POS allows not only for transactions to be recorded but for inventory to be adjusted for reordering. A computerized POS also allows for promotions to be entered, discounts to be recorded, and reports to be executed to help determine the effectiveness of advertising campaigns. This will allow you to document promotions and manage inventory, and it will help with bookkeeping.

Using the zip-codes in the coupon code is one way I keep track of redemption in a geographical area. For instance, our store zip-code is 93710, with neighboring zip-codes of 93711, 93726, 93720, and so on. When a coupon is redeemed, you don't always get the customer's address upon tendering, so you need to track it in a different way. Our coupon codes are based on zip-code, so if the customer brings in a Mother's Day coupon and lives in 93720, we use the coupon code "Mom93720." Now I know where that promotion worked, and how many times. You can never have too much information. This is a simple way of keeping track.

ROI

Understanding the term "Return on Investment" (ROI) is crucial. Whenever we advertise, we're looking for a good return on the money we dished out for that campaign. Most people measure this by an immediate return on their money. For instance, say you spend eighteen hundred dollars on a coupon in your local newspaper, and you redeem forty-five of these coupons, with an average ticket price of forty dollars. You look at that as a break-even; you received eighteen hundred dollars in sales for the same investment. This is the *wrong* way of looking at things, for more than one reason.

The first reason is that you must consider the cost of the goods. See the following.

Retail price of product	$49.99
Subtract the cost of product	$24.00
Gross profit of product	$25.99

If you run a gross profit margin of 50 percent (half of the purchase price of the product was gross profit), your cost of items sold was nine hundred dollars. Without removing other costs, like utilities and wages, you lost money on this venture.

The next erroneous viewpoint is looking at the eighteen hundred dollars as the only income you generated. This is incorrect. It is more appropriate to look at the quality of the forty-five new customers. Suppose that three of these customers become loyal customers who spend one thousand dollars per year in your store. This is called "life value"—you multiply the average ticket sales time frequency and the remaining years of your customer's life span.

CALCULATING A CUSTOMER'S LIFE VALUE

Average ticket sales	$83.33
Multiply by frequency	12 (This assumes monthly purchases.)
Multiply by years	20 (This number is based on the average age of your customer subtracted from the average life span. For instance, a forty-five-year-old customer with a projected life span of sixty-five years equals twenty years as a customer.)
Customer's life value to your store	$20,000

Now, what was your return? Great ad! You received $4680 from an investment of $1800, and that's just this year. Those three customers are going to return year after year and will spread the word, giving you the best advertisement, word of mouth.

All of your advertising must be geared toward gaining a quality customer with the potential of creating a loyal base. Do this and your ROI will be through the roof. You do this best when you target your specific demographic always within your immediate geography.

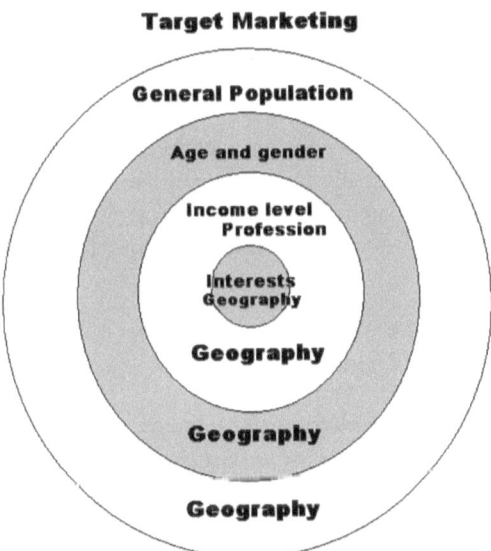

Target Marketing

General Population

Age and gender

Income level
Profession

Interests
Geography

Geography

Geography

Geography

WHERE CAN YOU GO FOR MARKETING TOOLS?

I learned that newspapers have an incredible marketing department you can use as your own. This is a huge opportunity for you. Your local newspaper has zip-codes, statistics, and mailing lists for anybody doing anything. Their marketing department is set up to do e-mail blasts, Internet banners, and printing and graphics to place in both direct mail advertising and newspaper inserts. Their professional staff can be yours, and you will pay for their services after designing a campaign. Newspapers' mailing lists usually require a fee but are readily available. Their graphics design team and expertise are all part of the printing costs. They usually have much better postal rates than you could come up with. This is all yours for the taking, so take it!

CREATING A DIRECT MAIL CAMPAIGN

- Purchase a mailing list from the newspaper, from InfoUSA (www.infousa.com), or from another source. Remember to use as many lifestyle filters as possible and stay close to your store geographically. Try to get a list of subscribers to trade magazines that would appeal to your potential customer.

- Create an offer with an adequate window of time for purchasing. Typically take into account the printing time plus mailing time and add your window to this. I like a two-week or end-of-month time frame.

- Call your local newspaper for an oversized, full color, two-sided postcard mailing based on your list quantity, plus two hundred extra cards. These extra cards are for bag stuffers in your store. If your newspaper does not have a direct mail department, you can use InfoUSA as a printer and mailer.

- Initiate the in-home delivery of the offer on a Thursday, in time for the weekend, which will generate higher sales.

I used our local paper's marketing department to acquire the subscribers list for a backyard birding magazine, *Birds and Bloom*. This magazine had three thousand subscribers in our area. The newspaper's graphics department created an oversized postcard to mail using my graphics and wording. Our offer was a free five-pound bag of seed. I strongly recommend pursuing this type of advertising! We redeemed nearly 20 percent of those coupons, with an average ticket price (ATP) of $70. Now, in reality, a direct mail campaign is considered a booming success if it gets a 2–2.5 percent return.

Why was this one campaign so successful? All of the recipients were well qualified. They all subscribed to the perfect magazine for our hobby; their interest was already established.

Many of these recipients also became loyal customers. Loyal customers are crucial to success. We need four hundred loyal customers to make a living in Fresno. One such customer will spend one hundred dollars a month on seed and supplies. Finding such individuals should be your goal, since they are the ones with a high life value. A well-targeted mailing list is a gold mine, so mine it!

SHOPPING FOR A RADIO STATION

- Schedule a meeting with them. Most radio stations are housed in clusters; for instance, Clear Channel Radio may have seven stations within one building. Meet with all of them at the same time. Doing this creates a competitive roundtable for all the stations vying for the sale. This often gets you a better deal.

- They will all hand you a folder with demographic information and statistics on their listening audience. Take this with you.

- *Never* buy time in this initial meeting. Wait a week. Make them sweat it out a bit and come up with a more attractive offer.

- Choose two of the best stations to broadcast with from *two different* parent companies. Doing this segregates the salespeople so they can't compare notes. This will create a bidding war for your business.

- Play the companies against each other. Compare their ad's creativity, air time, listening time (ideally, you want commute time, especially the evening commute), on-air personalities for the live remotes, and on-air giveaways, etc. Tell one that so-and-so is giving you such-and-such; can they match the offer or better it?

- Remember that the listener needs to hear your ad at least three times before they even notice it, so frequency is very important.

I scheduled radio spots on a soft rock station for the week prior to and the week after the store's grand opening. We also had a live remote for that Saturday—something I recommend. It created a carnival atmosphere, which in turn built excitement. The DJ said he had never seen a more successful grand opening than ours. In addition, we gave gift cards to the radio station to use in on-air contests the week of the opening. If you choose to advertise on radio, make sure you pick the station whose audience is your demographic, not necessarily the station with the music you like best.

No, I didn't stop there. I had the newspaper create an 8 1/2 x 11 full-color insert for newspapers in the immediate zip-code and the two neighboring zip-codes on the Thursday prior to our grand opening. Thursday had the widest circulation with little competition in ad space and immediately preempted our weekend event. This was expensive and gave us the worst return on our investment, but it still wasn't bad, since our redemption was 2.5 percent of the total number of inserts.

CREATING FREE WORKSHOPS

- Determine what workshops would promote sale of your goods.

- Find appropriate instructors. Preferably, you could instruct, or if you need help, as I did, you can solicit a local club or nonprofit organization to lead the workshop. They love the added exposure. You can even offer a donation for their time.

- Mention the workshops in your advertising. Post this on public community boards. Include this in your press releases. This will be covered in detail later, in chapter six.

- Create and prepare a comfortable area for the event.

- Serve refreshments.

- Make sure you appear and introduce the workshop even if you are not conducting it. Your participants need to see who you are and associate this service with your generosity. See Appendix C.

Schedule events and workshops for your opening. We had birds of prey brought into the store (courtesy of the zoo and the local rehab organizations), story time and puppet shows, a bird walk (led by Audubon Society members, who guided the forty-five people who showed up), gardening for birds (conducted by a master garden club member), giveaways, and much more. Balloons, balloons, and more balloons! You have to create a carnival for people; this is crucial!

Our store was packed from wall to wall that weekend, and although we did not set any records in sales for the franchise, my family and I were very pleased. This success reassured all of us that opening the store was a good idea.

Now, I did set a $5,000 budget for grand-opening advertising, which I exceeded by $1,200. *Not good!* The success of our opening created in me some pride and a little too much confidence, as you will see later in chapter five.

Nonetheless, our successful grand opening was the result of very good targeting of our prospective customers through filters that sorted out interest in our hobby, like the *Birds and Bloom* magazine subscriber list. Attaching ourselves to prominent and respected local organizations gave us credibility and made the press release important to the media, creating a much greater impression with higher visibility. Finally, utilizing the resources of an established marketing department helped me make better use of my time.

4

Up and Running

Off to a good start, and with the success of our first press release, I decided to do another release detailing our neighborhood bird walks. This got us another full-page spread in our local newspaper in full color. I took a reporter and a photographer on a bird walk right behind the store in the park. Three northern flickers (a very pretty woodpecker) made a guest appearance, which mesmerized my guests. They were excited traveling back to the newspaper to write an article—the best advertising you can ask for.

Press releases are a *must* for success in advertising on a budget. They don't have to be incredible, just noticeable. For instance, this one got us a small mention in the local paper.

For Immediate Press Release

Contact: Wild Bird Center
Michael and Katherine Ruffino
Owners
Wild Bird Center
1075 E. Bullard #107
Fresno CA, 93710
559-432-WILD

The "Corner Store" is Alive and Kicking!

(5/11/06—Fresno, CA)—Fresno's Wild Bird Center brings the old way of doing business back to Fresno.

Today's retail world has evolved to a bottom-line mentality. Customers are numbers and are seldom truly appreciated. The day when the owner was in the store, smiling at all who came in and treating them as friends are all but gone.

Michael and Kathy Ruffino wanted to reintroduce what we all wanted but companies forgot to give, so they opened the Wild Bird Center here in Fresno.

Michael has worked in large "big box" stores for sixteen years and has seen what retail has sunk to. When you come into the Wild Bird Center, you truly feel welcomed. Refreshments are served to the customers as a courtesy.

The Ruffinos also don't believe in expiration dates on coupons. Michael states, "Putting an expiration date literally turns away a customer when they finally do pick it up. Turning away a customer is poor business, and retail has forgotten how to accommodate their livelihood."

As for return policies, "The answer is yes!" Michael continues. "Putting restrictions on returns can be viewed as insulting. The customer who has a problem with their purchase should not be treated like the plague."

Knowledge about what and why we all should buy something is rare these days. Although Michael is a relatively new birder, you wouldn't guess it when talking to him. Classroom training, bird walks, and computer-aided training has fueled his passion for this hobby.

The Wild Bird Center also has an array of activities for all ages. It offers free Saturday bird walks and children's activities throughout the summer, creating a culture in which this store is more than a store; it is a community resource for all. They even bring their activities to the classrooms.

It is comforting and refreshing to see that "the customer does come first," and even more than that, that they are befriended.

Notice that the format is always the same, and the quotes make it seem that I was interviewed. You can have a lot of fun with this; you're the reporter interviewing yourself—now, that's fun! Use items like new birds in your area, bird walks, store events, community outreach programs that you're doing, or anything else that makes your store unique and fun.

However, with this press release I broke an unspoken rule of advertising: expiration dates. It's true I do not put expiration dates on many of my coupons. Why? Have you ever picked up a coupon only to notice that it has already expired? And then what do you do? Well, I throw it away and either look for a valid coupon or wait until I get another. What a waste of money! You paid money to get the message out, only to turn away a sale. There are times I do put expiration dates on coupons—like for clearance sales or seed sales—but for the most part I do not. The experts get on my case about this, but I simply disagree with them.

What happens when you don't put an expiration date on things? I mentioned the *Birds and Bloom* direct mail earlier, which did not have an expiration date on it. Most of the coupons were redeemed during our grand-opening festivities because of all the hoopla. But, many have been steadily redeemed, even to this day, nearly two years later, and the coupons are still in immaculate condition. These customers probably put the large coupon on their refrigerator for all their friends to see during this entire time. Is that bad? *No!* Did I get more for my money in this case because of not having an expiration date? *Yes!* Their friends and family saw the coupon also.

In your marketing you have to think like the consumer you are targeting.

- Will *you* read or hear the advertisement?
- Would *you* use the product presented?
- Is the message important to *you*?
- What about *your* shopping experience?
- Is the store comfortable and inviting?

All these questions have to be answered for the ad to succeed.

CATERING TO THE CUSTOMER

Why don't department stores have a pool table in the women's department for the men who are dragged in by their wife? The stores know the husbands are trapped there, waiting for their wives to emerge from the dressing room. Husbands just stand around trying to look cool in the middle of the lingerie section. We should be considered. With that in mind, at our store we have a Kid's Corner—a specialized department with children's products and an activity center to occupy the little ones.

ACCOMMODATING FAMILIES

Some stores in our industry have no Kid's Corner. In my opinion, that is a real mistake!

As I mentioned, our primary demographic is females between the ages of forty and sixty-five. What is the most precious thing to grandparents? Grandchildren!

Catering to these little ones is important to our customers. From occupying the child while Grandma shops to giving her ideas of what to buy her little one, this department pays for itself more than any other.

Some stores think of this department as wasted space because it doesn't sell product out of its space as other areas do. Think of these truths:

- The area occupies the kids while the parents or grandparents spend more money.

- It brings in the parents, a demographic we have a hard time drawing in. How? When Grandma brings Junior in, the child has such a good time that he or she tells Mom and Dad. And then guess what happens? Mom and Dad also come into the store.

- A lot of our press arises from our children's programs. We have received one hour of network morning show time and sixteen inches of column space in the newspaper just this year because of the children's events. Translate that into actual sales, and you have a worthwhile department.

- We have marketed ourselves as a resource to the community. Part of this is because we have children's programs like puppet shows, story time, and crafts. Our children's department is set up to convert to a simple theater and to conduct activities in the room, including an entire wall for children to draw on with chalk.

- You also have to consider that if the children are not occupied with what *you* want them to do, what will they occupy themselves with? Little hands can make big messes.

- Ignoring children is shortsightedness. As our demographic ages, we have no reserve. Plus, the kids are cute and so much fun.

If you don't like kids, get over it! You are the one missing a big boat of opportunity.

Your store should cater to the needs and concerns of the customer. I'll tell you that if the local department store had a pool table in the women's department, I would shop with my wife more often. The fact that we cater to the little ones allows grandparents or parents peace of mind; it shows a genuine concern for their children's happiness and education. Even we have peace of mind, because we know where the children are and what they are doing. This fits perfectly into our marketing philosophy of being customer-centric.

Sending out press releases has continued to prove fruitful for us. Remember that your customer has needs and concerns beyond the purchasing of a product or service from you. Accommodating those concerns when they shop shows an unusual interest in them and builds loyalty beyond what they give to your competition. This attitude and service builds loyal customers. Being different helps the media pay attention. Don't blend into the retail world; give the media a reason to write a story!

5

Don't Let Them See You Sweat!

As I mentioned earlier, I got a little too full of myself when it came to advertising. If it worked once, I figured, then I should do it again and again.

My last company sold high-end electronics, and the power of video as an advertising vehicle was greatly exaggerated in my mind. One prominent public speaker preaches about the death of mass marketing. He insists that mass marketing gives a terrible return on investment. For the most part, I have come to agree with him on this.

Sales continued to crescendo our first year. February was better than January, March was better than February, and so on. But the problem with opening a niche business in a new market is multifaceted. You have *no idea* what market acceptance or business trends will be. The market is in the dark about who and what you are. Since there were no existing statistical data for the local economy established by similar businesses, all I had to go on were the indices (market trends) that the franchise gave me. According to those, June was traditionally the second-best month of the year, second only to December, of course. As June approached, my excitement built, and I saw an opportunity to cash in on the crescendo.

With this trend in mind, I developed an advertising plan for May and June, working my advertising around Mother's and Father's Day. I contacted NBC to create a local television commercial with regular spots during peak hours for the two weeks prior to each holiday. The commercial turned out to be a masterful piece, exactly what was needed to send the right message to the public—or so I thought. All in all, this TV campaign cost just over $5,000.

I went to broadcast TV to reach a wider audience, thinking it would create a better return on my investment. I could not have been more wrong!

I then thought that since I had gotten a good return on my newspaper insert for my grand opening, I would do so again, in 50,000 newspapers in three zipcodes. This cost me about $1,800. Well …

We also advertised on radio, with giveaways for the same time period, which cost $1,000.

Then I fell for the Internet banner pitch. The local newspaper asked me to add a banner on its Web page for "only" $300 per month, with a three-month commitment. I didn't think that was much, since they said a half a million people would see it monthly. *Wow!* What a deal! Uh, no, actually—bad idea!

WHEN SETBACKS HAPPEN

Sales did not continue to crescendo; in fact, they crashed. Evidently, all the goldfinches left town. This was the bird to which everyone enjoyed feeding about ten pounds of seed a day. Customers went into a goldfinch withdrawal. I was new to this hobby, and I was caught unawares by this and did not know what to do.

May had 25 percent less gross revenue than April, and June was 25 percent lower than May. I spent money thinking things would turn around in June. The crescendo was supposed to swell to a triple forte in June, but it was as though the orchestra stopped playing. To top it off, in July we had the worst heat wave on record, with temperatures topping 114 degrees for fourteen days straight. July was even more miserable for sales. This was a truly deep financial hole I had to climb out of.

If and when you dig a hole, just remember there is always a ladder. The trick is finding the first rung on your way up. In this case, starting with a padded bank account would have been nice, but as you can see, my confidence in my past experience and abilities led me to believe I wouldn't need the extra funds. I hope that, with the help of this book, any hole you might dig will be shallow enough that you can just step out of it.

It was at this point I decided to get creative. With no money left, I had to get the word out about our little store as you will see in the next chapter there are ways of advertising for little or no money.

After what can be deemed the summer from hell, with sales plummeting to half of what they were in May, I had to make the ultimate sacrifice, my Charger. If I could put tears on this page, I would.

Financially speaking, this turn of events might have folded our business if I hadn't had an investment I loved as much as a person could love anything inanimate—my '69 Dodge Charger. I restored this car from junk in a span of six years, rewiring it, doing body work, painting it, and installing a new engine, new transmission, suspension, and on and on. She was a 575hp mean machine that I put my soul into.

This situation may happen to you more than once; it happened to us three times in our first year. It caused more stress than I had ever felt before. At times, I was near tears. My entire life, money, and resources were wrapped up in this venture. I had never before had so much to lose.

Never Let Anyone See You Worry; It Is *Your* Worry, Not Theirs.

If others see your fear, then they will fear. If your customers and employees lose confidence in your ability to make your store a success, your failure becomes a self-fulfilling prophecy. If you think you will fail, you will!

Hide your fear well! To all those around you, make it seem as though things could not be better.

To be mentally tough, a person must see past shortfalls and recognize what is possible. This isn't a bunch of hooey; it is a fact! Mental toughness is found in people who have a healthy diet, a good workout regimen, and an optimistic disposition. I once heard a talk entitled "Stepping Stones, Not Stumbling Blocks." The emphasis of the talk was on seeing opportunity where others see failure. One story I loved from the talk was about Hall of Fame quarterback Joe Montana in the huddle. The team had just been scored upon and was down by less than a touchdown with a minute and a half to go in the game—to top it off, their backs were pinned against their own goal line. Joe got in the huddle, looked at his offense, and said, "Okay, guys, we got them right where we want them." The players all broke out in laughter, and Joe drove the team down the field and threw for the winning touchdown. He turned a stumbling stone into a stepping stone, recognizing an opportunity where others perhaps would have seen failure. You must see past the failure, look for solutions, and create a positive outcome from setbacks if you are to survive.

So you made a mistake. It happens! In my own instance, I had really made a mistake. I didn't budget in line with a credible forecast. I spent way too much money on advertising. As if that wasn't enough, I also stocked my store to my forecast and had those bills to contend with.

But I was forced to look past this problem of heavy debt and no money. Tough, you say? Yes, it was. Learning that not all markets are the same and that Fresno's market had its own signature trends was an important lesson.

I let my successful grand opening create in me an unbalanced enthusiasm that clouded my judgment. This is easy to do, especially after an emotional high. You will fail at times, but learn *why* and *how* to avoid the same mistake again, and then you will have made a costly mistake pay off.

I have come to understand the reality that the new business owner is the definition of being mentally tough. By creating a positive atmosphere in your store for both your customers and staff, you will be able to ride out those tough times. Your customers and staff will all feel safe and secure in the thought that you and your store can continue to cater to their needs in the distant future. You will also see in this next chapter that the small business owner has to be creatively frugal when need be.

6

Advertising with Little or No Money

What to do? We were broke and living day to day. Kathy went to work full time, a first in her life, in order to help pay the bills. I had to come up with a marketing plan with no budget. Impossible? Well, I thought so at first, but necessity is the mother of invention, a statement no truer than in the situation I was facing.

This following list describes what I did to survive and thrive under difficult circumstances. You will get a lot of good use from this list. Attaching yourself to events and organizations is a great way of riding on their backs while they promote themselves, thus trickling the promotion down to you. Doing so also allows you the opportunity for a very meaningful press release. The Internet, again, becomes a great resource to make this happen.

TWELVE WAYS TO ADVERTISE FOR PENNIES OR FOR FREE!

1. ***Community Calendars:*** I listed our bird walks, children's shows, and so on. These calendars are free, and they attracted the customers that used them.

2. ***Internet Message Boards:*** You can find these by going to a site like Yahoo and doing a search for your hobby. Join the message board and post all of your events on it, with reminders three days prior to the event. The boards automatically do an e-mail blast for your event.

3. ***E-Newsletter:*** At only $18 a month, this one's as good as free. We started to acquire our customers' e-mail addresses in order to set up an e-newsletter. We use www.constantcontact.com. Why? They have tem-

plates for your use and incredible security for your customers' addresses. Security is something everyone is concerned about when sharing any information about themselves.

4. *Flyers:* Yes, there is the expense of photocopying, but it is minimal. We created a business flyer offering a staff discount to neighboring businesses. We personally visited each business and brought a gift. In our case, I took a puzzle that cost $3 per item. It was a nice token of our appreciation. We then printed enough flyers to go door to door in our immediate neighborhood, and we put them on car windshields. Again, some would frown on this practice, but it worked. You have to get bold—and in my situation at the time, I was bold.

5. *Press Releases:* You already know what these can do for you. Release at least one every month. Use the example press releases in this book to help you format your own. The title should be striking enough to draw interest in the content. The content should be direct, to the point, and not too wordy. Give people a reason to investigate the announcement. Who do you send the release to, and how? In short, send it to everybody! Go online and look up every local television station, newspaper, and radio station. Each of these outlets has contact information pertaining to press releases. Put all of their addresses in your e-mail manager, in a folder titled "Press Releases." Now, whenever you write a press release, you can just send it to everyone in this folder. Be relentless. The media outlets will not respond to all of your announcements, and perhaps not even half, but they will respond to some. The exposure you receive is phenomenal!

6. *Off-Location Events:* Let schools know you are available for in-classroom instruction. Volunteer at nonprofit events. Join the Wildlife Rehabilitation organization or any other respected group in your area that's relevant to your store. Use all these events for press releases.

7. *Creativity:* When we put the offer out to schools about in-classroom training, we were inundated with requests. You might wonder, how could I be everywhere at once? I came up with the answer: a short film! Yes, I created an on-location puppet show about owls, titled "Owl Be There." This project was very affordable: $50 for the software, $38 for a hundred DVDs and cases, and eight hours of my time for shooting and post-production, which I did on the computer. Now I can be in a hundred class-

rooms at the same time! The film also made for a great press release, plus we sell DVDs of the film in the store to recoup our investment.

8. ***Your Local Parks and Recreation Department:*** Get in touch with your city government and find out how to volunteer for summer programs or speak at senior citizens' centers. This can get you in the city's good graces, and you will be surprised at all the free press they get; you can ride on their backs with this.

9. ***Private Retirement Homes:*** We offered sit-down bird excursions at city parks. These are simple; they're held under a park gazebo, and we show seniors the wildlife around them. This idea was readily accepted by the homes. Now, if your demographic is not the elderly, then look to youth organizations or women's clubs. By reaching out to them, you create a good reason for the media to pay attention to you.

10. ***Secular Observance Days:*** National Bird Feeding Month and Earth Day are our opportunities for outreach events. Schools, nonprofit organizations, colleges, and universities all have press for their events. Latch on! Congress has mandated all sorts of observances for virtually every day of the year. One or more may fit your demographic.

11. ***Walkway Newsletter Stand:*** We publish a franchise-mandated newsletter, which we offer free by mail and in the store. But how can a passerby get one when the store isn't open? We attached a newsletter holder to the outside handle of our door for after-hours customers, who simply help themselves to the newsletter. This has worked well.

12. ***Window Bulletin Board:*** In our window there is a bulletin board advertising events, current birds at feeders, and the most popular mixes. People will rely on this board in your window.

The nice thing about owning your own business is that *you* control your outcome.

You need to be aggressive if you expect to survive. Stress can be high, but doing nothing constitutes giving up, and it creates even more stress. There is a reality I have never faced before: I have never failed at something major. Perhaps this will happen sooner or later, but it will not happen now, not on this!

DO NOT BE AFRAID TO FAIL!

If you're not failing at tasks, you're not trying hard enough!

You can tell from my failures that I *was* trying. I love the way PepsiCo thought outside the box on the issue of failure. PepsiCo once instituted a policy for managers to mandate an amount of failure to further success. What? Well, it makes sense when you think about it. If you don't fail from time to time, you will never get better; you're not trying hard enough. When PepsiCo mandated this, they removed the fear of failing. Consequently, some of their best policies and ideas arose from this action.

It is wiser, though, if you fail at things that don't cost too much.

Here's my pep talk. You will fail at tasks, but you are not a failure. If anything, you are better than those who never tried hard enough and settled for mediocrity. Your failure at a specific task was a victory, given the fact that you learned a great deal from it.

When these bumps arise in your road, hit the gas pedal. There is always a solution to the problem just over the hill.

FINDING HELP

- If you are a member of a franchise, ask other franchisees about how they overcame the problem.

- Join the Chamber of Commerce, where other owners gather and can help you through these rough times.

- Always hold out hope. I said this once before: if you think you will fail, then you will.

To accompany all of the low-cost promotional events and avenues mentioned above, you must budget for other advertising. In the next chapter you will learn the what, where, and when of buying advertising.

This book is designed to help you succeed more often than you fail, which creates a lot less stress. In this chapter you have found that a smart marketer doesn't need to have a lot of money, just a lot of creativity and effort—but most of all, a smart marketer is *never* passive. Don't be afraid of failure; welcome it! We usually learn more through failures than successes. Remember that there is more than one way to promote your business and create revenue. By thinking creatively and taking advantage of mediums that are free, such as the Internet, you too can compete on a shoestring budget.

7

Buying Advertising

In the end, "marketing" is just a sterile word to describe the fact that you are giving people a reason to purchase. The best form of marketing does not focus on products at all but on experiences. Yes, if you discount something, it will bring in those who were planning on buying it anyway. Alternately, you can sell an experience. If the experience is enticing enough, it will draw people in just for that experience, whether they wanted to buy or not.

In sales we used a saying, "Sell the sizzle, not the steak!" Big companies do this all the time. In a recent Bank of America ad, you see a window shaped like the Bank of America logo, suspended in a downtown metropolitan area. As people walk by, they peer into the window only to see themselves fulfilling their dreams, wishes, and fantasies. That is selling the sizzle!

The general public wants to be wow-ed! We want to experience something new and exciting. We are bored with shopping. The average store presents us with nothing new in product, atmosphere, or buying experience.

I recently took my family down to Disneyland. Why is Disneyland, Disneyland? Because of the *experience*! They set the stage perfectly, from the front gate to standing in line, something we all hate anywhere other than Disneyland. There, standing in line is the start of the ride.

Our store environment should be part of the ride of purchasing. When we designed our store, we made sure that it stood out from all other stores in Fresno. Imagine stepping into a storefront and onto a river rock path with clouds, treetops, and butterflies flying overhead. The sounds of water cascading and birds chirping create the illusion of a park. The walls are painted with murals of treetops, nesting birds, and flying indigenous birds of our area. This is our store. When we advertise, we accentuate the overall experience and sell the store as a must-see. Yes, we specify what we are and where we are, but the emotional grab is the overall environment. We simply "sell the sizzle." This brings in people out of curiosity; even if they wouldn't come in to buy a feeder, they come in because they are curious.

It doesn't take much for you to do this. You sell a product that fills a need, and with the fulfillment of that need comes a favorable response. Sell that response, that emotion! When people buy in this way, price is not an issue. Their hopes, dreams, wants, or needs are fulfilled—and you made it possible. These customers become loyal customers, returning again and again, because of what you did for them.

The common question is how much you should put into your budget for advertising. Well, this all depends on the success of your advertising. A failed ad costs you a lot and takes away from future marketing ventures.

**Set aside about 5 percent of your gross revenue
to market your new business.**

When creating an ad, we shouldn't create a culture of discounting. We immediately want to give a certain percentage off to entice the buyer, but if you do this often enough, your customers become used to receiving a discount and thus wait for the next ad. They may even think you're overpriced because you can discount all the time. Killing this monster you created is difficult. If you choose to discount, do it intermittently and with a good size break in between the ads.

A NEW APPROACH TO ADVERTISING

Instead of discounts, try a new approach to hook customers: give something away. Just take a moment to think about this. What is a better draw: something for free or a discount? Free, of course. Which can make you more money? If you're thinking the discount, you would be mistaken. It would depend on what you give away.

I am in the bird-feeding business; I was originally duped into giving away five pounds of seed. This brought in people, but many came in just to get the free seed and nothing else. So what had to change? What if I gave away a feeder? That way, I would be creating a need to revisit the store, for additional seed. I would also be forcing the customer into a purchase of seed at the time of the giveaway. In addition, I would have created a larger impression by giving away a durable product. Would I make money? Yes! When I give customers their feeder, which costs two dollars, they in turn by a five-dollar bag of seed. I make a profit of $2.50. I netted fifty cents if they buy nothing else, but it's likely they will buy about forty dollars of merchandise, which is my average ticket price. So, for the cost of the ad and two dollars for the free feeder, I just reaped an average of about eighteen dollars in profit per visit. I also created a possible loyal customer because of my generosity.

By giving things away, we create a reputation of generosity, not discounting. We also create a need in the marketplace if we give away a product we supply the needed accessory to—in this case, feeders needing seed. This is a home-run campaign!

Now that we have talked about what to advertise and a budget to guide us, we now have to make a choice. With all advertising mediums there comes commissioned salesperson to sell you on the fact that their advertising medium is the best in town and the best for you. Just today, three radio station salesmen have contacted me, all saying the same thing: "We are the best for your store!" Just remember, they work on commission.

CREATING A GOOD RETURN ON YOUR INVESTMENT

When choosing an advertising medium, you must first gauge its effectiveness through its established filters and the ability to track the outcome. This is necessary for determining the return on investment (ROI).

For instance, television, through individual channels and shows, creates a filter for a specific listening audience. Advertising on ESPN will target mostly men, the Food Network mostly women. The difficulty with television is that it's nearly impossible to track its effectiveness, and it requires a substantial monetary commitment. These variables affect your returns on the investment. In the following list, the ROI is relative to the cost of the promotion. In choosing, consider whether you could get a better ROI through a different medium.

ADVERTISING MEDIUMS OVERVIEW

- **RADIO:**

  —Good Filter—Tough to track—$$—Low ROI

  —The format of each station will target a specific demographic. If you choose this medium, I would suggest doing a live remote at your location. You should incorporate a free giveaway during drive times, as well. The radio station will give anything away if you offer it for free. I would recommend a gift certificate so that the winner will visit your store.

- **NEWSPAPER:**

  —Poor filter—Easy to track—$$—Low ROI

  —Because there is no filter to target a demographic, this "buckshot" approach to advertising has a low ROI.

- **TELEVISION:**

  —Good filter if you use programming as a filter—Hard to track—$$$—Low ROI

  —Because of the needed frequency and the costs of producing a commercial, this medium will produce some results, but at great expense. This creates a low ROI.

- **YELLOW PAGES:**

  —Poor filter—Easy to track *if* you insert a coupon—$$$, depending on size—Low ROI

  —I have come to the conclusion that the world has gone yellow. I simply cannot believe how many competing yellow pages there are per town. At first, I did not know their effectiveness, so I put a coupon in for a free bag of seed in order to track the ad. A total of 485,000 books were delivered, and I had only twenty-five redemptions, most of which came in just for the freebie. My obvious conclusion was that it wasn't worth the expense. However, if you have competition in your market, you should consider outdoing their ad in the biggest phone book for your area. Remember, though, that there is no filter, and your ROI is low.

- **DIRECT MAILINGS:**

    —**Internal Customers**: Great Filter—Easy to track—$$—High ROI

    This is a great revenue builder and a habit-forming way of marketing. During nearly every transaction you tender, you ask for the customer's address. You then can send customers a direct mail offer. This will bring them in, creating a habit of returning often. In my experience, this has a redemption rate of 20 percent or so. The plus is increased sales; the minus is that you're not increasing your customer base. These mailings should be balanced with other promotions.

- **Buying Addresses:**

    —**Trade Magazine Subscribers**: Great Filter—Easy to track—$$—High ROI

    Yes, you can buy an area-specific subscribers list for nearly any magazine on the market. As you know, we did this for our grand opening, and the redemption rate was through the roof. Make sure you pick the appropriate periodical for your business, then go to your local newspaper's advertising department. They will arrange everything for you. There is a cost associated with buying the list, on top of the actual mailings, but it's well worth it.

    —**Move-Ins**: Good filter—Easy to track—$$—Med ROI

    This is a nice form of neighborhood marketing. A move-in is what it sounds like: a family either buys a house or rents one and moves into the neighborhood. When you send the card, make sure it offers a "welcome to the neighborhood" gift the customer can pick up at the store. This has a very good redemption rate and inspires positive feelings in the recipient.

    —**Radius Marketing**: Great Filter—Easy to track—$$—High ROI

    What is this? Radius marketing is a fairly new and effective way to increase your business. Companies like SmartleadsUSA (www. smartleadsusa.com) or my favorite, InfoUSA (www.infousa.com), offer a helpful marketing tactic by targeting your existing customers' neighbors. You simply submit one of your customer's addresses to the company, and they then calculate the nearest neighbors and send out an oversized postcard informing the neighbors that the Joneses on Sycamore Avenue are enjoying such and such from your store. The postcard also presents an offer of your choosing, so the recipient can have the same experience as their neighbor. The target has a connection to one of their neighbors, and this neighborhood is obviously well suited for your demographic, which increases the likelihood of a high ROI. This is a good mailing to help grow your business.

The best way to assure a good ROI is to piggyback these promotional mailings with your internal customers. If you add a purchased list to your internal customer list, you will assure yourself a greater return on the investment while cultivating your current customers and still growing your business.

- **NEWSLETTERS:** Great Filter—Easy to track—$$$—Low ROI

  —Why low ROI? Because people see this mailer as either a valued piece of literature they do not want to cut up for the enclosed coupon, or they view it as junk mail.

  —Mailing a newsletter has become rather expensive and antiquated, due to e-mail options. After decades of taking great pride in authoring their own in-house newsletter, our franchise has decided to switch from paper to electronic media. Mailing a six-page newsletter costs me about $6,000 per year. Could I use this money more wisely?

  —A friend of mine just finished his postgraduate work, and in his thesis he analyzed our company newsletter. In his findings were some rather depressing and startling conclusions. Customers could not recall a single article in the newsletter only a few weeks after receiving it. They did not make purchasing decisions based on the articles, either.

  —Now, think of how our franchise felt when they saw these results. Mailing newsletters to customers was part of a culture dating back to the days of the first store. Seeing these findings was disappointing, to say the least. But, committed to keeping in touch with our customers and seeing the changes in the way people retrieve information, we decided to move from paper to e-mail. As you have seen in the previous chapter, this is an extremely cost-effective and very versatile medium.

WHEN TO ADVERTISE

Have you ever gone fishing? Where and when do you fish? Well, of course, where and when the fish are biting. You need to advertise during the general public's buying cycles. Do not try advertising during slow months, when all businesses are slow. Capitalize on holiday frenzies and seasonal trends. The obvious is the Christmas season. People are used to spending money during this time and to not capitalize on this trend would be unwise. The back-to-school period might suit your product line, or Valentine's Day. The secular calendar is full of celebrated days you can tie into a promotion; use them.

My whole reason for writing this book is to give you guidelines to create a better overall ROI. Marketing during buying times is just smart. You can try something during this period, like a happy-hour sale on weekdays. Usually we have slow times during the day, and designating a period just before the busy time for a sale elongates that busy time and capitalizes on a buying disposition.

TRACKING YOUR PROMOTIONS

Having a computerized POS system is of immense value. We use Microsoft RMS, but there are others out there. A good POS system offers you tracking at the touch of a button. In the case of promotions, you will simply assign a promotion code to each promotion. I usually attach a zip-code to each code to more easily identify sweet spots in our area. As I mentioned earlier, if I run a Mother's Day ad, I would assign it a code with several parts, like "mom0793710." This code actually tells me a few things: the obvious is "mom" for the actual campaign identification, then the year, "07," and last but not least, the zip-code, "93710." Pulling up a coupon report immediately tells me a lot at a glance. This saves a lot of time and makes the job of marketing easier.

Create a calendar of events and promotions. This becomes a sort of strategy sheet for the year. Next, create a file, and insert this calendar, copies of each promotion, and a coupon redemption report. Then you have the best reference money can buy for future promotions.

In this chapter we have considered the what, where, and when of advertising. The synopsis of different avenues is only a guide based on over twenty years of experience. Use this road map in strategizing your yearly budget and event calendar. Use holidays to help you schedule the events, for holidays are used as buying indicators within the retail world. Your marketing efforts must be ongoing and tireless in order to be effective.

In the following chapter we will discuss what to do when the customer walks into your location.

8

Maximize the Sale

What do I mean by "maximize the sale"?

It takes a lot to get customers through the door. All I want you to do is make sure you satisfy their wants and desires when they enter your shop.

A lot of business owners who open their own store do so with passion for the product mix and a desire either to make a worthwhile impact on people's lives or to make a lot of money. Yet what they don't realize is that it takes salesmanship to make a success of their venture. This applies to all financial endeavors.

Now, I have been working for a professional sales organization for sixteen-plus years. I have trained hundreds of men and women to be the best at their craft of selling. This does not mean taking every penny from customers' pockets or misleading them.

A great salesperson listens to the customers and then makes sure they get all they need and want in order to fulfill their wishes. This requires a bonding that evolves into a measure of trust.

FIRST, SET THE STAGE

- **Have a Clean Store**

    A clean store can not be undervalued. Your store directly reflects you. All areas should show your attention to detail, from the front sidewalk to the bathrooms. I have been in stores with the grossest, most cluttered bathrooms. The back office had the door open, exposing the remnants of a hurricane. What does this tell your customers? Stand at your entrance right when you open and ask yourself, "How does this look?" Why do this at the start of the day? As the day progresses, we become blind to our environment; thus, we have a fresh perspective first thing in the morning.

- **Create a Task Schedule**

  Create an opening and a closing task schedule and stick to it—yes, even you!

- **Merchandise Your Store**

  There is a funny truth about people when they walk into a store: 80 percent of them turn right. So merchandising your store should begin there.

  Merchandise your store in a logical pattern of shopping, where one purchase leads to the next in line. This makes selling and buying easier. Remember, anything below waist level will not sell. Chest to eye level is the sweet spot. All of your displays should convey a theme or message.

  Change your islands around about ten times a year. Your customers will think you bought a bunch of new stuff. Crazy! It keeps the store fresh and new.

- **Stimulate Customers' Senses**

  When new customers walk into our store for the first time, they are greeted by the sights and sounds of nature, including birds chirping and the sound of cascading water. They step onto an aggregate pebble path that leads them to their first purchase—a bird feeder; or, for children, the path leads right to the Kid's Corner. Each customer sees a world of possibilities they never dreamt of: the incredible selection of feeders, birdhouses, birdbaths, gifts, seed, and more seed. It is a lot to take in, and customers need the salesperson's help to sort through it.

  Be a gracious host to your guests. If they are welcomed, they will continue to return, becoming all-important loyal customers.

  Fresno has a hot desert climate, and providing ice-cold water for customers is inexpensive and has a high impact. Offer seating for the elderly in an area with background sounds, a video monitor, or books; you'll be surprised how well that goes over. Little things matter.

- **Offer Guidance to Customers**

  Owning a retail store requires you and anyone working in your store to sell merchandise. Sounds like a no-brainer, but it's true. A successful retail store sells well. What does this mean? Attachment sales! For instance, a person comes in for a bird feeder. Do you just sell him a feeder? *No!* A poor salesperson does. You show the customer the best seed to attract pretty birds. You show him different feeders for different birds. Where is he going to put the feeders? Does he need hardware, rain guards, or baffles? You get where I am going with this.

A great salesman sells more than what the customer came in for. Is this wrong? No! Most of the time, customers have no idea what they need to create their desired effect. Our job is to show them what is possible based on what they want.

THEN, GET A CAST

Finding good help is hard and getting harder. I have three requirements for employees to maintain their job with me. They have to avoid the "Three L's":

NO LYING, NO LAZINESS, AND NO BEING LATE TO WORK!

When employees avoid these things, you have honest, hardworking, and punctual employee. Easy? No!

Traits of a Great Salesperson

- A great salesperson is honest.
- He or she is hardworking.
- A great employee is always punctual.
- A great salesperson is a true extravert, a WOO-er (winning others over).
- This individual loves making friends.
- He or she has never met a stranger.
- This individual is at home in groups and crowds.
- Finally, this person needs to be passionate about what he or she is selling and enjoy doing it.

Where to Find a Great Salesperson

- They usually visit your store every month and buy something. Look at your customers first.

- People in the service industry, including waiters and waitresses, are great multitaskers and are used to pleasing a customer.

- Look at your competitors. I usually don't advocate stealing, but in this case, steal their best salesperson.

As for pay, don't be cheap! If you pay minimum wage, you will be fortunate to get an effort equal to that. Starting an employee out at a few dollars above minimum is wise and sets the expectation that the employee has to earn it.

You should also have a signature document outlining your basic requirements for the position. This would include your policies on tardiness, dishonesty, and insubordination. This last one must be spelled out so there is no fuzzy area. As for punctuality and attendance, this has been my number-one reason for firing someone. My tolerance is very low, but I realize tardiness and absenteeism do happen, so I make an allowance in this initial contract.

Having a signed document on file is the best way of holding someone accountable and, if necessary, terminating that person legally.

Give meaningful annual raises when warranted—none of these twenty-two-cent raises, which is a meaningless gesture to the employee. A good employee is worth a lot more than you pay him or her, so demonstrate your appreciation.

BASIC SALESMANSHIP

Every sales organization I know of teaches basic steps for a sale. It is a fact that people buy from people, not from companies. Ask yourself about the last big purchase you made. Why did you buy that product at that time? Were you comfortable with the process? Did you trust your salesperson's advice?

The best salespeople have the ability to transfer their enthusiasm to customers, creating an exciting experience, one that customers will readily tell their friends about. Eighty percent of all purchasing decisions are based on emotion, not intellect.

A good salesperson follows a certain natural progression to assure the customer's greatest satisfaction. These are called the five steps of the sale.

Steps of the Sale

Approach:

This is the most important step. It sets the stage for success or failure. You usually have about thirty seconds for this step; you need to greet customers within thirty seconds of them entering the store.

Do not greet from behind the counter if you're not ringing anyone up. Make eye contact and welcome the customer to your shop. Smile sincerely!

Try greeting the customer like an old friend you haven't seen in years. If you're a hugger, you can hold off on that until the customer comes in a lot more. Believe it or not, I do hug some customers as though they are old friends.

Ask the customer's name, and *use it*!

Never ask, "Can I help you?" A closed-ended question usually gets a "no" response. Rather, say "How can I help you?" Always ask open-ended questions.

Qualify:

This is the exploration stage to determine why the customer is in your store. Ask, "What brings you in today?"

During this step, I usually ask customers how they found us. This allows you to gauge the effect of hard-to-track advertising like radio.

Explore their dreams and help them see the possibilities. Let them do the talking. In this stage, you have control. Steer them to your recommendations, but let them step on the accelerator or the brake to slow down. They want and need your opinion, but prevent yourself from sounding like an interrogator.

Presentation:

Show customers your recommendations. Explain why you recommend the item, using the feedback you just received in the qualifying portion. For instance, "Joe, you said you wanted to attract goldfinches. With this feeder you will not only attract them, but you'll get the spectacle of seeing them eat right side up, upside down, and every-other-which way." Give them an easy second option to choose from; letting them have an element of control is essential for your customers' confidence in the purchase. For instance, "And this feeder will only allow the goldfinches to eat upright." Here is a difference that customers can understand, helping them choose.

Demonstrate the accessories you recommend and always tell customers the benefits of the accessories. Mentioning a feature without listing its benefit is meaningless.

Overcoming Objections:

This is easy: if you did the first three steps well, this step just won't exist. But none of us is perfect. Take ownership of the error—"I'm sorry, I misunderstood you"—and then go back to the qualifying step. It is very important that you hear the customer's objection, since you probably didn't listen well to begin with. Acknowledge the concern, and then you can move on to re-qualifying the customer.

Ask for the Sale: Oh no, not this!

There are two ways of closing the sale: hard and soft.

Me, I am a soft closer, the kinder and less aggressive approach. For instance, as I present products to customers, I simply start stacking them on the counter. If I am wrong, they will tell me. This is called the assumptive close, because you're assuming they are going to buy the item. In electronic sales I would always ask, "Would you like me to check stock?"

A hard close is, "Will you be buying this today?" or "How will you be paying for this today?" This approach is a pretty much an in-your-face way of asking for the sale. Some people are very good at this without sounding pushy or offensive.

These are the five steps of the sale. Get them down, and you will increase your average ticket sales exponentially. Train your staff on these steps and role-play with them. Watch them interact with your customers and then ask them what they could have done better. They know!

STACKING CUSTOMERS

This term is used for helping more than one customer at a time. It's a lot of fun but takes a little practice. To do this successfully, you must turn your back to the product and face the customers, allowing you to see the whole store. This is the only way to see people promptly as they come in, in order to greet them.

There is another matter I need to mention, too: never allow your mind to take on too many things at once. Those who have a problem with stacking have a problem with prioritizing thoughts. Give your attention to one thing at a time—in this case, just one after another. If you let your mind take on five different things at the same time, you will get flustered, and your customers will, too. Relax! Answer one question and then answer the next question, and so on.

The one thing we all want when we shop is attention. When you are helping several customers, it is important to ask their permission to attend to someone else, with the reassurance that you will return promptly to continue assisting them.

When you do this, make sure you give the customer something to do. Hand them a product so they can examine it while you are away. Doing this will make the time go by much faster; those two minutes you're gone will feel like seconds.

The rush you get from helping multiple customers is cool. I am at my best when I can stack four or five customers. You will also discover that all the energy you display generates excitement. This excitement will transfer to your customers, and they will be better disposed to buying.

Even behind the register, I can acknowledge a customer without neglecting the one I am ringing up. This can be done with a simple nod or "Howdy."

Smile! Smile! Smile!

CREATE A BUYING ATMOSPHERE

Having in-store specials can create a positive buying energy in your store. You can have a "Managers Special," a "Back-to-School Special," or even have each of your employees come up with one and name the special after them. Having employees create these specials creates a buy-in, a sense of ownership of the promotion that can be hard to come by. It also shows that you listen to them and take their advice. Whatever special you choose, make sure you decorate the store nicely, with appropriate signage and merchandising to support it.

Each special must be obviously special to create an impact. All of us have inventory that just didn't sell, and even discounting it didn't help, so what do we do with it? We have a grab-bag special from time to time, with raffle tickets in a bin. With each qualified purchase, usually exceeding a set amount, customers can reach into the bin and grab a free prize. We merchandise the prizes behind the register so customers can see what is there to win. We even mix in some really good items to entice them into upping their ticket value. This works really well, and you get to clean house while creating a higher average ticket.

PITFALLS OF THE SALESPERSON

Talking Too Much:

One of the biggest mistakes a salesperson makes is talking too much. When you ask a question, wait for the customer to respond. Control your urge to say something. This may take two, ten, or even thirty seconds, but the answer will come. This is difficult, especially for an extrovert.

My first sales trainer eighteen years ago thought I talked too much and too quickly, so she asked me to count to three after every response the other person made. Three seconds is a long time! What this taught me was to think before I spoke. The delay allowed me to digest the comments of my customer or even my friends. My subsequent response was more insightful and meaningful. I and my acquaintances owe a lot to a simple three-second rule.

Too Much Information:

Another pitfall is giving the customer too much information. When my last employer hired sales associates, they sent the associates through a rigorous training on electronics. I knew just about everything, from signal-to-noise ratios to the amount of time a proton took to scan a cathode ray tube (CRT). This training gave the salespeople confidence in their product line, which came out in their words and demeanor. The problem with the training, though, was learning to shut us up about all this newfound knowledge. We bombarded those poor customers with frivolous information they could care less about. We were trying to impress them into buying.

The plain truth is that customers don't need to know why something works, just that it works. If they ask why, tell them in simple terms, not technical terms. They don't want a tech sheet on the product. They just want it to satisfy their needs.

Don't Confuse the Customer:

The last pitfall is too many choices. Do not confuse customers with *all* the choices. Present two choices and no more! Each item should be markedly different so the customers can easily make a selection. This allows customers to have the control over buying that they want. Offering three or more choices only confuses buyers and forces them to leave and go somewhere else where they won't be confused.

By applying the five steps of the sale—offering a hospitable approach, qualifying the customers needs, giving a solid presentation, overcoming any objections, and then asking for the sale—you will take advantage of your traffic and do better than most start-up companies. Avoid the pitfalls of talking too much or inundating customers with too much information, thus confusing them. Remember, a well-trained and fluent salesman will bring in more money than the best ad ever could.

9

The Forgotten Facets of Retail

The operation of a retail store has many facets. We have talked about driving customers into our store and creating an inviting atmosphere, both in the physical nature of our shop and the personable nature in us and our staff. What about policies and answering the phone? What about an Internet presence?

RETURN POLICIES

As you have already read in one of the press releases, I have an open-door policy on this issue. Why? A return is a great opportunity to create a loyal customer.

My best salespeople always greet a return at the door with a smile. The customer carries in the item and discusses the reason he or she is returning it. The salespeople then start the five steps of the sale all over again. They realize that turning an unhappy customer into a happy customer is gold. To exceed these customers' expectation creates a loyalty second to none. You will also find that the reason they are returning the item is because the item did not meet their expectations and they need something better.

By posting return policies, you create a negative feel at the point of sale. It is at this point that all things should be positive and all the customer's decisions should be reinforced. Will some customers abuse this policy? Perhaps, but more will become loyal customers than the very few who take advantage of your generosity. You can always refuse service in the extremely rare circumstance.

PHONE ETIQUETTE

More and more nowadays, the phone is used for shopping and for asking questions. The way you answer the phone is critical. The goal is to get that customer in your store so you can properly help him or her.

First of all, answer the phone before the third ring. Now, most of the time I am in my store alone, so I have to carry the phone on my belt so I can answer it promptly. If you are with a customer, excuse yourself from the customer and get a comfortable distance away so your phone conversation will be private. Glance occasionally in the customer's direction, this will reaffirm to them that you have not forgot about him or her.

Next, *smile*! Why? Everyone can hear a smile. Try it. Close your eyes and have your employee or loved one say something to you, both with and without a smile. I guarantee you, you will hear that smile.

Try not to close sales over the phone; if you can, talk the customers into coming into the store. Getting them into the store allows you to maximize the sale.

If you say you will call them back, do so promptly at the first moment you can. This always impresses people.

HAVING A WEB SITE

You have to love the computer age. It's brought a wonderful new world of low-cost advertising on the information superhighway, the Internet.

Do you have to have a Web site? No! But it doesn't hurt, and it gives you a presence in a realm most people frequent. When we picked our physical store location, we chose an area that allowed the right people to find us with ease; a Web site should be similar.

Your Web site should reflect your store's personality. It should welcome your guests and exceed their expectations. One article I read stated that a Web site is a necessity for competitiveness in today's world. I wouldn't go that far, but I would agree that it is a wise choice. You would be surprised at how many people find you through the Internet.

When it comes to Internet technology, I have to admit my inadequacies. Yet I have found some fun ways of spicing up our Web site. If you visit our site, www.wildbird.com/fresno, you will find videos on many pages, including a video tour of our store created from snapshots in Windows Movie Maker. You will find a personal tour of our Kid's Corner with my little girl, Rebecca (my favorite video). There also is a variety of videos of birds and bird walks, with an instructional video on "dig scoping," and many more.

How did I do this? YouTube (www.youtube.com) is great; it allows hosting of large files with the ability to imbed the video's code directly in your Web site. It's free and easy—you've got to love it.

On our site you will also find podcasts of funny dramas, like old-time radio shows. I love nostalgic radio, so I write and produce comical audio skits with birds as characters. All these podcasts allow me to draw customers to our Web site and in turn teach them about nature. Our listening audience numbers into the thousands and spans the globe; we have listeners from over twelve countries. I use Podbean (www.podbean.com) as our Web host, which provides important documentation of my listening audience. This Web host also teaches me how to imbed our podcasts on other sites and promote them on iTunes and other popular sites.

If you want to sell merchandise on the Web, you can do it easily. Mind you, competition on the Web is intense. The overall idea of our site is to bring customers to the store. I believe that this should ultimately be your goal in creating a site.

A lot of companies out there will help you set up a site. Make sure your site is as simple as possible. Fortunately, our franchise offers site set-up as part of our package with them, and the software makes it easy for me to add and modify to my heart's content. The franchise also pays for top search results with Google and Yahoo, among others. These are just a few factors to consider when deciding to join a franchise or not.

Bottom line, if you drive customers into a poorly run business, the results will be poor. As you have seen in this chapter, even our policies have to be customer-centric. Phone etiquette is crucial in continuing to drive in new customers, as is any Web page we may have set up. All things reflect on us, and all things reflect on our bottom line: sales.

10

Budgeting

Without a set budget, you are doomed to failure!

In this chapter you will find a common-sense and practical approach to the concept of budgeting.

GOOD ACCOUNTING REQUIREMENTS

- Hiring an accountant for tax purposes, and
- Having an accounting program for your computer, like QuickBooks.

When we opened our store, our goal was that Kathy would do the bookkeeping and all of the budget calculations. Yet, as you have seen, things didn't work out that way. I figured if I just ordered what we sold, that would be enough. Uh … Nope!

My first year was what I consider a disaster on many fronts, accompanied by many successes. I did not budget the store's inventory and expenses properly. Mind you, I used as my excuse, "How can I budget without knowing the trend or having a baseline?" Now, how do I feel about excuses? Yep, I still catch myself making excuses sometimes.

FORECASTING SALES

Forecasting in the early years is near impossible unless you are opening up a second store in a nearby market, and even then you will find differences between the locations. Acquiring a reliable market index is difficult. You could contact a franchise that is operating stores in your market and see if they can give you this information. Becoming a secret agent doesn't hurt, either. Visit similar businesses in the area and strike up a friendly conversation with the owner to milk him or her for information. Retrieving this information is a huge advantage, but if you're like me, I did not have nor could I get any information for my niche business in this specific market. In such cases, you then have to rely on a larger statewide or national index for market trends.

Creating a worst-case scenario is a good and safe way to start in your first year. Your grand opening, if it was promoted well, will tell you how well your market has accepted you. Your marketing must be relentless. In your first year, you will be guessing a lot about what your next month's gross sales will look like. This can be frustrating. So, guess conservatively. For instance, if you conservatively estimate that next month your store will sell $10,000, make a budget based on that figure. You can always order more merchandise if needed.

Your second year will come with a great sigh of relief: you made it! You now think you have a baseline to help you project and forecast accurately, but ... not really. Your first year—no offense—was dismal in sales and at best may give you an idea about product mix ratio to overall sales. This then gives you a very loose idea as to monthly trends in sales. The good thing is that your hourly and weekly sales trends are fairly consistent. You will see what your busiest hours and days are so you can staff appropriately.

Still, you are left with some guesswork regarding purchasing. By examining last year's trends, along with the current month's sales, you will be better able to forecast next month's sales.

OPEN-TO-BUY (OTB)

Understanding a budget control called Open-to-Buy (OTB) is essential for staying within your means. The OTB formula is a way to budget inventory replenishment. This formula pertains *only to physical inventory* and is just one piece of the overall budget. Thirty-five percent of companies filing for bankruptcy are profitable. They simply did not manage their money well.

Still, if all ratios stay the same in your second year, then calculating your open-to-buy is fairly easy. Yet all things seldom stay the same, especially in the early years of a business. As your store continues its accelerated growing period, you will discover that your demographic settles into purchasing your core inventory.

Here's a good example of this. When we opened our store, our mix was heavy in feeders and then gifts. As business grew and settled, our mix became what it should have been, seed first, then feeders, and gifts last of all. I had to spend a lot more on seed and curb my spending on gifts. If I hadn't adjusted in this way, I would have created a debt I would've had a hard time recovering from.

Analyze your product ratio monthly, and use a rolling twelve-month period as your guide. This is crucial to accurately buy inventory. If half your sales are in one category, then half of your budget will be spent on that category.

OTB is a fairly simple formula: Planned Sales plus Planned Markdowns plus Planned End-of-Month Inventory minus Planned Beginning-of-Month Inventory equals Open-to-Buy (retail).

Planned Sales
+ Planned Markdowns
+ Planned End-of-Month Inventory
– Planned Beginning-of-Month Inventory
= Open-to-Buy (Retail)

For example: you start with $85,000 of inventory, and you plan on $40,000 in sales, with an expected discount due to a sale of $800. To Calculate your expected discount, start by estimating how many tendered coupons you expect against your average ticket sales; for example, you send out 10,000 flyers and redeem 2 percent, equaling 200 coupons, with a discount of 10 percent on an average ticket of $40, equaling $800 [10% of 200 × 40]. You need $90,000 of inventory going into next month. Here is what the calculation looks like:

Planned Sales	$40,000
+ Planned Markdowns	$800
+ Planned End-of-Month Inventory	$90,000
– Planned Beginning-of-Month Inventory	$85,000
= Open-to-Buy (Retail)	$45,800

You can download an Excel spreadsheet of this formula with future month projections at http://retail.about.com/od/merchandisingbuying/a/open_to_buy.htm. This is from the Web site www.about.com, and if you go to the business and finance section of the site and look under retail, you will find a wealth of information. Using the tools on the Internet is an advantage our parents never had.

> For your overall budget, create a spreadsheet using your expected gross against cost of goods and expenses. In other words, Gross Sales = (Cost of goods + facility expenses).

You have control over several of these issues; the obvious one is cost of goods, and, to a degree, your facility expenses like utilities and even payroll.

In this spreadsheet, break down your product categories, and then set a spending limit for each category based on your projected sales. For instance, say my gross sales will be $10,000. My facility expenses are $5,000, so that leaves me $5,000 to spend on product. Seed is my mainstay, so I spend half on that, then feeders at $1,500, and then hardware at $500, and miscellaneous at $500. This calculation assumes I have no payroll and I sell at a 50 percent markup. This budget is a simple breakdown, but it makes the point.

Projected Gross Sales	10,000
Rent, Utilities, Loan	– 5,000
Seed	– 2,500
Feeders	– 1,500
Hardware	– 500
Gifts and Misc.	– 500
Balance	0

Now, I have created a spreadsheet in Microsoft Excel where I input my purchase orders when they come due, and the expenditure is totaled against the budget. This really is pretty simple.

STAY WITHIN BUDGET!

Remember that we deal usually on a net-thirty term (which means that the bill comes due thirty days after receipt of goods), so you're budgeting for the following month from now. In other words, in May you're buying for June; that's when the bill will be paid. Be careful about extended terms, which can trap you if you don't keep them in that future month's budget. To help keep me from falling into this trap I have created a year-at-a-glance document that simply lists totaled bills due against that month's projected budget. This keeps me aware of what the future holds.

As I have said before, I knew nothing of birds and migratory patterns when I opened this store. I joined message boards on bird-watching that list sightings of birds so I can be ready for the influx of new feeder birds. I have learned that all bird species send out scouts ahead of the major migration, so when the first sightings occur, I have two or three weeks to set up shop for these. Pretty handy, huh!

In retail, December is the busiest month of the year; thus, your budget must accommodate the increased sales. I used the state indices from our franchise to get an idea of the logarithm for our store. As the years go by, you will see your store's own unique footprint in your local market.

It is important to stay within your core products in the first few years. Your core is the identifying inventory for you, the reason most people come in and the message of your advertising. In our case, it is bird feeders, birdseed, birdhouses, birdbaths, and binoculars. An example of what not to do was when my last company wanted to sell computers. They set up a department and bought computers. What a disaster! Low margin and changing technology caused recent purchases to become antiquated and obsolete. This created a mess and a loss of revenue. They quickly discontinued this department to focus on their core once again. The smart thing about this decision was it came at a time that they could afford to take a risk.

You cannot afford to risk leaving your core inventory for the first few years. The money just isn't there to lose on the risk. Keep your core inventories at 80 percent of your mix, leaving the remaining 20 percent to product, creating a unique footprint for your store.

You will also find that when you open your store, every salesman comes a-knocking, and I haven't heard one yet who wasn't convinced that his or her line wasn't the best on the market. You have to learn to *say no*! Stay within the budget. Salespeople will return, believe me. I always use the phrase, "We're a new store; you know what that's like." Works every time.

Understanding where you are and where you are going in terms of your monetary commitments is crucial. It's really not too complicated. In every aspect of running a retail store you must take deliberate steps, understanding where your foot will land. The OTB formula is a way of making sure your steps land on solid ground. Remember:

Planned Sales
+ Planned Markdowns
+ Planned End-of-Month Inventory
− Planned Beginning-of-Month Inventory
= Open-to-Buy (Retail)

Remember to stay within your budget and discipline yourself to say no to salespeople.

11

Working for Yourself

"It must be great working for yourself, with all that money." So states the ignorant observer. I have to admit that it is better than working for somebody else, but I am the toughest boss I ever worked for. The expectations I have for my store are high. I am naturally competitive, always measuring my efforts against last month and last year. As for the money comment, I'm laughing right now!

"You get to make your own hours and have all that free time." So states the really ignorant person. Customers and the store itself make an incredible demand upon your time and life. As you have seen in this book, the stress and day-to-day operations can consume you. Owning a small business should not be viewed as a liberating venture from time demands or stress.

CREATING A CULTURE

A culture is an environment conducive to sales. Creating the right culture is not hard. We have already discussed hiring the right people and setting the stage within our store. The five steps of the sale, when implemented with sincerity, create a culture in which the customer feels relaxed and ready to buy.

• You Are Your Culture

Culture inevitably reflects *you*! You dictate this in ways you are not aware of. For instance, if you manage people with an iron hand, how does that get communicated to the customer? If you keep a messy store, how does the customer feel about your environment? If you are in a bad mood, how does that affect others? You can see how *you* have a lot of power in this area.

- **Testing Culture**

A good or bad culture is seen immediately upon entering a place of business. One exercise I do all the time is to look at the faces of employees in the place I walk into. If they are not smiling or if they're displaying an unpleasant disposition, I know the manager is at fault. The supervisor is directly responsible for the employees' overall state. If I were a district manager, I would take all my employees aside and try to discover what was wrong, because something is wrong when employees are unpleasant. Look at your waiter or waitress next time you go out to eat. Do they greet you with a smile, are they informed about the specials, and do they know their menu items? If all these are checked off, you will probably leave a sizable tip.

- **Pricing: A Product of Culture**

This brings me to the point of price. What are people willing to spend for your product if the service and the culture are so much better than everybody else's? Probably more. We as consumers determine our expenditures based on several things—first and foremost, service. In almost every case study and focus group I have seen, the number-one thing a customer wants is intelligent and friendly service. Price is always third or lower on the list. The proper culture will allow you to compete with other stores that might even be cheaper than you.

- **How to Maintain a Good Culture**

Here is an exercise that you will find a bit scary. A long time ago, when my previous employer was heavily influenced by the firewalker motivational guru Tony Robbins, we were taught how to change our state of being. Here is the crazy part: by yelling in a crescendo the word "Yes!" over and over again while clapping our hands every time we said it, we were able to change a dull state into an excited state. I know, I know what you're thinking: that's crazy. But it works. When I would catch myself upset after a large return, I would go to the break room and start this chant, and I came out ready for the next sale. *It works!* Try it just once and you will see that you can't be sad when you're yelling "Yes!"

The Rewards of Owning Your Own Business

For me, having my own business is its own reward. My children, Rebecca and Russell, get to help out in the family business. At seven years old, Rebecca is the official manager of the "Kid's Corner," and Russell, who is only three, is the official "re-merchandiser" of everything below waist level. I get to bring our family dog to work, which she loves, and so do the customers. I look forward to the day I can hand down this business to my children and let them enjoy teaching people about nature.

Although the store needs to support our family financially, it is just as important that we make a profound impact on all of our customers, both old and young. This is the most rewarding part of operating our little store.

Running your own business is a lot of fun once you get the hang of it. Expect to turn a corner in your second year to break even. This, though, only comes with diligent planning and relentless determination. Some have wondered where I get all my energy. I have to admit that I do not know. Yet running your business can be a lot smoother if you only learn from owners like us and what we went through.

Do the things listed in this book, and you will not only have fun, but you will also make a profit!

Be SMART in all aspects of running your business.

Advertising is a must but does not have to be expensive.

    Attach yourself to respected organizations.

    Create a monthly press release schedule.

    Orchestrate in-house and off-location events.

    Stay within budget.

    Always do the free things balanced with the costly marketing mediums.

Maximize the sale:

    Make sure the stage is set.

    Follow the five steps of the sale.

    Greet customers like an old friend you haven't seen in a long time.

Create, and stay within your budget!

APPENDIX A

Creating a specific, measurable, attainable, realistic, and time-managed goal:

- First, come up with an ultimate goal.

  _____

  _____

  _____

- Then, think about what needs to happen in order for that goal to become a reality. There may be several things that have to fall into place; list these. These are now your secondary goals.

  _____

  _____

  _____

- You then have to look at each of these secondary goals and break them down, reducing them to their simplest component.

  _____

  _____

  _____

- Now, you create a step-by-step process for accomplishing each component.

  _____

  _____

  _____

- Create a timeline for each of these processes; the secondary goals will fall into place as these processes are accomplished.

  _____

  _____

  _____

- Do not forget to have check-ins so you can gauge progress and adjust any plan to new circumstances. Creating a flexible plan reduces many frustrations.

  _____

  _____

  _____

- As each of these tasks are accomplished, your ultimate goal will be realized.

  _____

  _____

  _____

Now display this sheet somewhere you will notice it.

APPENDIX B

SMART Goals Exercise:

Evaluate each sample goal below to determine whether it is a SMART goal. Is it specific? Measurable? Attainable? Realistic? Time managed?

I want better profits in two months so I can pay my bills.

[NOT]

I want to increase my invoice totals by 5 percent by the end of this quarter. This can be done through suggestive selling and better merchandising. Impulse items will be set up at the cash register, and training will be conducted on how to step up a customer to a more expensive and more suitable item. To aid the salesperson in this, the nicer product will be located near all advertised and lower-margin pieces. I will schedule myself to listen to my sales staff to aid them in this area.

[SMART]

I want to become a lawyer next year through diligent study.

[NOT]

I want to become a lawyer in ten years. I first need to attend college for my general requirements and Bachelors Degree, which will take five years. I then need to accomplish post-graduate schooling at a reputable law university over the course of three years. I then have to pass the bar exam to begin an apprenticeship at a law practice for two more years before starting my own practice or joining a partnership.

[SMART]

I want to increase the response to my advertising, thus creating more profits.

[NOT]

I want to create an ad campaign. I will do a direct mailing to four thousand qualified prospects through a leads company. I will filter the criteria to fit my demographics and mail within a three-mile radius of my location. The mailer will be a coupon so I can track its redemption with an expiration date within two weeks of hitting the homes.

[SMART]

I need to do inventory by the end of the month.

[NOT]

I need to inventory my store by January 31. We will close early on the 20th at 3:00 p.m. and start inventory at 3:30, after instructing staff on how to inventory each area. The store will be divided up in zones and counted twice by two teams, using adhesive dots to mark their progress. The inventory then will be entered and reconciled of all differences. The store will open at noon on the 21st in order to allow for any time needed to finish the counts on the following morning.

[SMART]

Appendix C

Creating Free Workshops:

- Brainstorm a workshop that will promote your sales and offers practical information:

_____

_____

_____

- Find appropriate instructors. Preferably, this could be you, or if you need help, as I did, you can solicit a local club or nonprofit organization to lead the workshop. They love to help because of the added exposure. You can even offer a donation for their time.

_____

_____

_____

- Mention this workshop in your advertising. Post information about it on public community boards and include the information in your press releases.

_____

_____

_____

- How would you word a teaser about this workshop in your press release and advertisements?

_____

_____

_____

- Serve refreshments.

_____

_____

_____

- Make sure you appear and introduce the workshop, even if you are not conducting it. Your participants need to see who you are and associate this service with your generosity.

_____

_____

_____

References

First and foremost, I recommend *Mental Toughness* by Dr. James E. Loehr and Peter J. McLaughlin; you will not regret purchasing this series of tapes and book. It will help you push through the trials of business ownership like no other. The book is not a bunch of hype but offers practical counsel to help you build a toughness you have not yet discovered.

The 10 Minute Marketer by Tom Feltenstein, who is a foremost leader in neighborhood marketing, will provide even more ideas.

First, Break All the Rules by Marcus Buckingham and Curt Coffman is a great tool for managing and for discovering your strengths. You will benefit from the book's information and in-depth polling by Gallup.

I recommend *Coaching Illustrated* by Mark David. I love a straightforward approach, and this is as straightforward as you get on the topic of management.

The One Minute Manager by Kenneth Blanchard, PhD and Spencer Johnson, M.D. Again, this is a straightforward, easy read to help you effectively manage people.

Web Sites:

StoreTech Services: This is a point-of-sale system designer and distributor. Contact them at 877-378-3316, or visit them online at www.storetechservices.com.

www.infousa.com—This is a great marketing resource. Buy filtered lists and create direct mail campaigns.

www.about.com—It's a very informative Web site, especially on the topics of business and finance. For an Excel spreadsheet, see http://retail.about.com/od/-merchandisingbuying/a/open_to_buy.htm.

www.sba.gov—This site has a lot of great information, not only on setting up your business but also offering helpful guidelines for running your business and obtaining needed capital.

www.wildbird.com—This is our franchise site and has information about starting your own Wild Bird Center.

www.constantcontact.com—See this site for your e-newsletter and other electronic communications.

www.smartleadsusa.com—This site offers information on automated neighborhood direct mail campaigns.

www.youtube.com—This will host your video and is easy imbedded into your Web site.

www.podbean.com—Use this for hosting your podcasts and detailed informational reports for your listening audience.

www.wildbird.com/fresno—This is our store Web site. Visit it, and you will get an idea of what is possible.

wildbirdcenter.podbean.com—This links you to our podcast Web site.

Glossary of Terms

Attachment Selling: The art of adding more to a purchase by recommending needed accessories.

Average Ticket Price (ATP): This is the average sale rung up on the register.

Budget: A monetary structure that dictates spending of given ventures.

Core Inventory: The product and services that best describe your store. This is the bulk of your product inventory. This inventory is the primary reason people come to you.

Culture: The overall atmosphere or feel of an environment.

Customer-Centric: All things center on the customer: attitude, merchandising, atmosphere, policies, and product.

Demographic: The Who, what, and where of your key customers. It describes the category of people who are your key customers, the target when you advertise.

Etiquette: The art of being courteous and polite, affording dignity to the listener.

Forecasting: The ability to identify trends before they happen.

Indices: Market trends and historical performance over any given time.

Insert: This is a loose-leaf ad distributed within a newspaper.

Life Value (of a customer): This is what a loyal customer will spend over his or her life span in your store. It is calculated by your average age demographic subtracted from the average life span and then multiplied by your average ticket price times the number of visits annually over that period of time.

Loyal Customer: This is a lifetime customer, one who will regularly visit and buy from your store. Finding these is your goal in marketing.

Market Trends: The buying cycles of consumers.

Merchandising: The art of displaying your product in an enticing and logical manner.

Net Terms: Payment terms of vendors. Net 30 indicates a payment is due within thirty days of order.

Networking: The ability to use multiple organizations and people to promote your venture.

Nordstrom Model: In this model, the customer is not just always right but is always deserving. Do anything to make the customer happy; exceed their expectations.

Open to Buy (OTB): The formula to help project future inventories based on sales trends.

Point of Sale (POS): A computerized system to maintain and manage inventories; a cash register; a sales tracker.

Product Mix: This is the ratio of categories in your overall inventory.

Remote: This is a live radio broadcast from your location.

Return on Investment (ROI.): This is the profit or loss from an advertising campaign.

Salesmanship: The ability to persuade another individual to agree with your viewpoint and act on it.

Soft Opening: An unadvertised opening of your store. Good for getting your bugs out and to test location effectiveness.

Stacking Customers: The skill of helping more than one customer at a time while keeping everyone happy.

Step-Up Selling: The skill of creating value in a more expensive product, convincing the customer it is the wiser purchase.

Vendor: A supplier of goods.

WOO: Winning Others Over.

978-0-595-47241-3
0-595-47241-9

www.ingramcontent.com/pod-product-compliance
Lightning Source LLC
Chambersburg PA
CBHW030411290526
45785CB00004B/1965